VICTORIAN AND EDWARDIAN DULWICH

FRONT COVER: Dulwich Village.

Toll Gate in Winter.

VICTORIAN AND EDWARDIAN
DULWICH

BY
BRIAN GREEN BA (Hons) Dip Hist

BARON
MCMXCV

FIRST PUBLISHED BY BARRACUDA BOOKS IN 1988
REPRINTED 1990
REISSUED BY BARON BIRCH FOR QUOTES LIMITED IN 1995
PRODUCED BY KEY COMPOSITION, CHENEY & SONS
HILLMAN PRINTERS (FROME) LTD AND
WBC BOOKBINDERS

ISBN 0 86023 432 0

CONTENTS

ACKNOWLEDGEMENTS

Without the help and enthusiasm of a number of people the compilation of this book would have been impossible. I am particularly grateful to Margaret Slyth and Austin Hall at Dulwich College Library for their generous assistance, often at short notice and inconvenient times. Similarly I am indebted to Nicola Smith and Stephen Humphrey at the Southwark Local Studies Library for their help and patience over many visits. I commend all readers of this book, and those who wish to pursue the history of this part of London further, to visit this library, which is within the John Harvard Library, Borough High Street, SE1.

Gladys Harrop kindly allowed me the use of early records of Dulwich Hamlet School and Giles Waterfield gave some valuable information on the Dulwich Picture Gallery. David Waller provided a number of important facts relating to the history of public transport in Dulwich and two members of the Dulwich Local History Group, A. Taylor Milne and Hilary Rosser, were most helpful in supplying information on the residents of several Dulwich houses.

Like many other authors whose wives have become involved in the progress of their books, I too am grateful for the encouragement and help of my wife, Rita, who has been a recorder of information on countless expeditions to various repositories of material.

The use of photographs from a number of collections is gratefully acknowledged: Alleyn's School, Dulwich College, Dulwich Picture Gallery, Dulwich Hamlet School, James Allen's Girls' School, Greater London Record Office Photographic Archives, Minet Library, Horniman Museum, London Borough of Southwark Local Studies Library. The following individuals kindly allowed me access to their collections: Bill de Baerdemaeker, Arthur Chandler and Len Girdler.

Bibliography & Sources

Blanch, W.H. *Parish of Camberwell* E.W. Allen 1875
Church, R. *Over the bridge* Heinemann 1955
Dulwich Society *Kingswood* 1985
Dulwich Society *Belair* 1986
Dyos, H. *The Victorian Suburb* Leicester University Press 1965
Green, B. *Dulwich Village* Village books 1981
Green, B. *Around Dulwich* Village Books 1982
Morris, T. *A short history of Dulwich Village* privately published 1909
Rogers, W. *Reminiscences* privately published 1895
Romilly, J. *Diaries* 1836-7 Cambridge University Library Add. MS. 6804
Ruskin, J. *Praeterita* Hart-Davies 1949
Young, W. *History of Dulwich College* privately published 1889
Wren, M.A. & Hackett P. *James Allen, a portrait enlarged* privately published 1968

The Greyhound.

For further research, reference to the various editions of Ordnance Survey maps of Dulwich, published from 1868 onwards will prove useful. The author's thesis *The history of Education in Dulwich 1619-1882,* copies of which are available for reference at the Southwark Local Studies Library, Dulwich College Library and the University of London Library, gives much detailed information on the growth of schools and of Dulwich College in particular. It is also a useful guide to manuscript sources.

Extensive use has been made in this book of the *South London Press* between 1865-1909 and similarly of the *St Barnabas Parish Magazine* 1893-1909. The *Dulwich Hamlet School Magazine* also provided much interesting information. Great use has also been made of the various census returns, published at ten-year intervals from 1841-1881.

INTRODUCTION

There is a curiosity about the past, about where one lives, who the former occupants of your house were, what they did for a living, why they came to Dulwich, what their children were like and what they did in their leisure time.

Those seriously interested might investigate further and their quest will lead them to study old street directories, poor rate books and census returns. They will consult wills and scan old newspapers, sort through countless accumulations of material in many places. It will be a fascinating and sometimes rewarding search. This book attempts to be a window into a Dulwich of the last century, how it developed, and why. It may prompt the reader to further inquiry.

Until the mid-1850s, Dulwich remained in more or less rural isolation. Agriculture was still the most significant industry, supplying London with the produce of its market gardens and milk from its farms. The fierce 'competition' between the railway companies led to Dulwich being criss-crossed by their tracks, and numerous stations sprang up. This new accessibility, combined with the enormous rise in London's population, signalled the end of agriculture as a major business and commenced the metamorphosis of Dulwich, from rural backwater to dormitory suburb. A handful of small dairy farmers survived into the present century and some of the wealthier new arrivals played the part of country gentlemen and kept model farms at Kingswood, Belair and elsewhere.

Dulwich developed at a different pace and in a different way to East Dulwich. The role of the College was instrumental in determining both the pace and nature of this development. During the 19th century more and more elementary schools were provided for the poor and the Great Schools existed for the wealthy. Between them was a void created by the decline of the grammar schools in the preceding century. Dulwich College, therefore, attracted the sons of the expanding middle-class, drawing its pupils from the newly created South London suburbs. The governors attempted to pursue a policy of providing second-grade education for the middle class, but were out-manoeuvred by the Master and the wishes of the parents. It was not anticipated that the lower classes would proceed to university and places for the Foundation scholars ceased in 1882. In some ways, Victorian society had retreated from some of the enlightened ideas of the 17th century.

The reader will find much reference to class in the text. In Victorian times class boundaries were rigid. Mrs Ruskin, living on Herne Hill, would not let John play with his Croydon cousins, because their father was a baker who lived over the shop; nor would she visit her husband's partner's family in case she felt inferior.

However, all through the period there was upward pressure from the aspiring lower classes to better themselves, intellectually, financially and socially. The numerous strata of what were termed labouring, industrial, working and middle classes all flourished in Dulwich. Houses were built to accommodate their social aspirations, and churches for their religious inclinations. Clubs and societies were formed and the period evoked a sense of determination and purpose.

ABOVE: High Street, Dulwich Village c1902. The newly built Crown & Greyhound on the right stands on the site of the old Crown Inn. Notice the bicycle rack in the right foreground, and the lady cyclist! BELOW: Horse trough at the cross roads of the Village, East Dulwich Grove and Village Way.

11

OPPOSITE ABOVE: The High Street and the corner of Turney Road. CENTRE: The row of shops in what was called Commerce Place, tucked away behind the towering elms. BELOW: The Village cross roads, looking towards Calton Avenue. The White House on the corner was the home of the blacksmith Richard Evans. On the opposite corner stands a fire alarm. ABOVE: Richard Evans, one of the Village blacksmiths, outside the forge which stood on the site of the row of shops in Calton Avenue. BELOW: The White House and forge seen from Court Lane; on the right is Ash Cottage.

ABOVE: Court Lane; on the left are the gates of 'Eastlands' and on the right the gates of the new Dulwich Park. BELOW: Ice being delivered by cart in Court Lane.

14

ABOVE: High Street, Dulwich; on the left is Burgess's, one of the Village butchers. This old shop was rebuilt in the same style in 1936. BELOW: The Crown Inn 1890. This village inn had earlier catered for the thirsts of Dulwich's agricultural workers.

16 *ABOVE: The Greyhound, Dulwich's premier coaching inn and venue for many of the Village's social gatherings. BELOW: It was a popular destination for excursions from the more crowded parts of London.*

ABOVE: The Fountain was erected by grateful villagers to commemorate the sixty years of dedicated service given by the Village doctor, George Webster, from 1815-75. The plans for the fountain were laid before his death. INSET: the old sweetshop patronised by the boys from the College. BELOW: After it was demolished it was replaced by the bank and a new shop.

ABOVE: Christ's Chapel, in the centre, the almshouses on the left, and the old College on the right. BELOW: College Road and almshouses. OPPOSITE ABOVE: Early days and BELOW: Victorian elegance, in College Road.

College Road, Dulwich.

ABOVE: The Chapel, Chaplain's garden, from the Picture Gallery garden. RIGHT: Gardeners at work in the Picture Gallery garden. BELOW: The mausoleum containing the remains of the Picture Gallery's benefactors — Noel and Margaret Desenfans and Sir Peter Bourgeois. The lantern top was to provide the inspiration for the design of the ubiquitous telephone kiosk.

20

ABOVE: Pickwick Villa, College Road, the house, legend has it, that Dickens chose for Samuel Pickwick's retirement. BELOW: Lovers' Lane, also known as Pensioners' Walk, linking College and Gallery Roads. The parkland on the left was known as The Grove.

ABOVE: Oakfield and the cross roads at Dulwich Common. BELOW: Allison Towers, Dulwich Common, stood on the corner of Allison Grove and was built in 1868, the architect, Philip Lee of Pimlico. Shortly after, it became a private military academy, with Herr Woolenhaufst, a former captain in the Prussian army, as principal lecturer. Thirteen students aged 18-20 boarded there, eight of whom were lieutenants in the militia. OPPOSITE: The Millpond, Dulwich Common: on 10 January 1891 it was reported that an enormous eel had been killed in a pond in Dulwich. The water was entirely covered with ice and, a hole being made, the eel came to the surface in a comatose condition, and was taken out without difficulty. It was 3'9" long, 11" round the thickest part and weighed 9lb.

Dulwich Common.

24

VICTORIAN GROWTH

Between 1820-60 development in Dulwich was limited to the occasional building of a house, cottage or a village shop. The reason for this might well have been the inertia of the College, the self-governing body which was landlord of almost all the 1,500 acres of Dulwich. Sufficient income was already being derived from rents to provide the Master, Warden and the four fellows with a comfortable income.

There was, however, considerable building along the north side of the ridge of Herne Hill, which became popular with the rising middle class, drawing such residents as the Ruskin family. Here, the frontages were narrow and the gardens long. Here, serpentine paths wound mysteriously through abundant shrubbery. The houses on the south side, overlooking the Dulwich valley, were more spacious and frequently had the convenience of one or more fields on the steep slopes behind them, to allow their occupants to graze their horses.

In the 1840s a suburban elite had established itself on Champion Hill and formed a residents' association, to supervise lighting and the maintenance of its own gravelled road, the mark of social detachment.

Dulwich itself was becoming less fashionable at that time. Whilst at the beginning of the Victorian period eight wealthy families employed a governess, twenty years later there was only one such family. Nor was the exodus from Dulwich confined to the wealthy. The population declined from 1,904 to 1,632 between 1841-51. It does seem, however, that the average age of the inhabitants was getting younger as, in the same period, the child population showed only a slight decrease.

The picture in East Dulwich at the time was similar to the neighbouring hamlet of Dulwich. There was a cluster of large mansions in the vicinity of Goose Green and a small development of terraced houses in Frogley Road and Nutfield Road, but there was no stimulus as yet for the intensive development which was to come. Access to East Dulwich before the arrival of the railways was difficult. There was no way the prospective residents could travel to and from their place of work.

All was to change, however, and the effect on East Dulwich would be cataclysmic. If an attempt is made to date this watershed, then 1854 would make a good starting point. In June of that year the Crystal Palace opened, bringing employment to hundreds and entertainment to thousands. It had the odd effect of making the surrounding area fashionable, odd in that few people today would relish living next to Disneyland, for instance. Not everyone welcomed the Palace. Ruskin, for one, hated it, but the prosperous and rising middle class, who were making their fortunes as merchants in the Empire or purveyors of goods which 'modern' Britain considered indispensable, found the area desirable. Of course, there was the benefit of the surrounding Dulwich Woods and the handy railway from Sydenham to Town which may have attracted some.

Other railways followed over the next ten years and, for the speculator with a store of capital, the opportunities created by their arrival were irresistible. There was one further factor; the population of London was growing at a much faster rate than the rest of the country and many were living in congested parts of the City in which a growing number of business houses wished to expand. The people therefore migrated to the suburbs; the better-off the individual, the further out he went. There was a desire to live in clean air and near green fields. The green fields of Dulwich were soon to be reached and, in East Dulwich, engulfed by the human tide.

East Dulwich in the first half of the century was in the hands of only four landholders. The largest of these was the Friern Manor Farm Estate, which comprised some 200 acres of farmland between Barry Road and Peckham Rye and was bounded to the south by Woodvale. The estate was snapped up by the British Land Company in 1865.

By 1868 the future shape of East Dulwich had been determined. Roads were marked out but were left unsurfaced and unnamed. A few bolder building speculators took plots from the freeholders and built the odd partial terrace of four or eight houses. A walk through the roads of East Dulwich today will reveal a mixture of styles, as different builders erected what they considered would appeal to prospective tenants. In Barry Road, no less than 49 different builders were involved in house construction.

The terraced house sought to bear an outward resemblance to the grander mansions of the more prosperous residents, living in detached and sylvan seclusion on the hills around Dulwich. Ornate porches and bays became a mania and plasterwork fruit and flowers competed with the occasional grotesque or regal head above the front door. Brickwork was often incised or laid at an angle, and use was made of two-colour brickwork to enliven the façade. Gable-ends on larger houses were often elaborately fretted and there was extensive use of coloured glass on front doors and their surrounds as the century progressed. Some developers dubbed their terraces with titles and individual houses received what their builders considered appealing names.

Most of the houses in East Dulwich were rented at between £30-£60 per annum for a seven-room house with bathroom and garden. Eleven per cent of the occupiers owned their freehold homes. Many of the absentee landlords were private individuals with some spare cash for investment. For example, Joseph Harris who, in 1880, lived at Oakfield in College Road, Dulwich, bought a plot of land to the south-east of Ildersley Grove in West Dulwich, and erected Gorleston Villas, naming his development after the place of his birth in Suffolk. Oakfield Cottages in the same road also bore his stamp.

The peak years for building were 1868-9, 1878-80 (when construction was three times greater than in other peak periods) and 1898. The years in between saw little building activity. There was difficulty in letting completed houses: of the 5,000 houses erected in East Dulwich between 1871-81, 1,000 were empty and, of the remainder, many were only partially let.

One of the causes of this was that, despite the fact that railway stations existed at convenient points, the actual number of trains stopping was few. As late as 1888, a complaint was made that, whereas only 37 trains stopped at Champion Hill (East Dulwich) on weekdays, the number stopping at Rye Lane (Peckham Rye) was 246! Much of Dulwich was ill-served by road transport. In 1884 the failure to let many houses in the district was blamed not only on the bad roads but on the absence of public tramways. Trams were not to penetrate Dulwich fully until 1906-8.

In Dulwich proper, the reorganisation of the Alleyn Charity by the Act of Parliament of 1857 required the building of new schools, and this more or less coincided with the expansions of South London's railways by the various railway companies. This windfall of railway money was soon exhausted by the governors' plans and other ways had to be found to increase the College's income. To this end, therefore, the College embarked on a programme of development of its estate. This development was controlled by Charles Barry Junior, who had succeeded his father as the College's Surveyor. Under his guidance the Governors were selective in the granting of building leases and at first confined development to the edge of the estate, in an effort to preserve Dulwich's now appreciated leafy isolation. Barry, who lived at Lapsewood, Sydenham Hill, and several other Governors living in Dulwich, were clearly anxious that it should not become just another densely populated suburb, as was happening all around its borders. The continued use of toll gates, long after most of London's had been swept away in 1865, discouraged those using the area as a convenient through-route, although the gate on Court Lane was blamed for deterring development in the adjacent area of East Dulwich.

Sydenham Hill, Sydenham Rise and Crescent Wood Road were developed and further new roads were made in West Dulwich: The Avenue (Dulwich Wood Avenue) and Victoria Road (Dulwich Wood Park).

In the centre of the village, the number of shops was increased by the filling-in of the old Long Pond, and a small development took place in Elms Road (Gilkes Crescent). The Governors, no doubt at the behest of their Chairman, William Rogers, also encouraged the building of cottages for the poorer classes, and the Dulwich Cottage Company erected a row in Calton Avenue and another at the end of Boxall Row.

Allison Grove, which stood on land outside the Governors' control, began to be developed in 1870, much to the distress of its neighbours. More houses were built there in 1881, the rentals for these nine-roomed houses ranging between £40-£60. College Road became lined with substantial houses at a rental of £120 and its prospective tenants were advised by the estate agents of the day that, for shopping outside the local facilities, the proximity of Sydenham Hill station opened up such areas as Penge, Herne Hill or Loughborough.

Another early development which was only partially carried out was the Dulwich Manor Estate, leased from the College by F. Doulton MP. Palace Road (Alleyn Park) and Alleyn Road were laid out and some houses built between 1862-6, but this development was interrupted by the financial difficulties encountered by Doulton. The roads were completed twenty years later by another developer. The manor house itself was demolished to make way for the row of shops at Park Hall Road and the southwards extension of South Croxted Road.

27

Edwardian development in Dulwich occurred following the demolition of the Greyhound in 1898, and the subsequent clearing of Garden Row, part of Lloyds Yard and Boxall Row, collections of old tenements in proximity to the inn. For a time, the Greyhound's cricket fields were let to sports clubs.

At North Dulwich, the death of the widow of Thomas Lett, who owned Dulwich House and its extensive grounds near North Dulwich station, caused the trustees to sell the land on building leases for the carefully controlled development of Beckwith, Ardbeg and Elmwood and surrounding roads, with houses costing not less than £400 each. By 1901 the population of Dulwich had risen to 10,961. Building land was usually sold at auctions held at local public houses. The Grove Tavern was a favourite venue, but occasionally the vendors would hire large marquees in which to conduct the sale. One such event took place in 1895, when the remaining plots of the Townley Park Estate came onto the market. By then all the open fields had been sold, and the old mansions with their extensive grounds were coming under the hammer.

At this particular sale, which took place in March, the weather was cold, and coke fires had to be lit inside the tent to keep the temperature above freezing point. Altogether 250 people were present, and bidding was brisk. By the end of the day, 57 of the 64 lots offered were sold; the price for plots of 17' frontage averaged £86.

The reasons given for the phenomenal growth of development in Dulwich in 1895 were the same as estate agents extol today — educational facilities and the beautiful park. The activities of speculative builders were bemoaned at the time. In 1904 a writer in a local magazine complained, 'The field in Court Lane where we used to play is now practically closed to us, a row of houses being rapidly erected there', and a year later another writer said, 'Within the last ten years a marked alteration has occurred. On every hand suburban walls are taking the place of green fields and with the increase in facilities for travelling the olde world appearance of Dulwich Village will undoubtedly disappear'.

Photographs here and overleaf show the development of Dog Kennel Hill from ABOVE: a pleasant country road with the old toll house on the left in good repair to BELOW: the arrival of the navvies and the widening of the road.

HILL, ROAD AND LANE

ABOVE: The laying of the tram tracks under the railway bridge at East Dulwich station and BELOW: the arrival of the trams down the steep side of Dog Kennel Hill in 1906. The number of tram tracks was later increased to four, for safety reasons, so that no trams would follow each other on the same line. Although other instances of four-line tracks occur in the British Isles, Dog Kennel Hill was the only permanent arrangement, and has a place in transport history.

30

ABOVE: This footpath across the Five Fields from the Village to the Plough, Lordship Lane, became Woodwarde Road. By 1896 it was gaslit from end to end. BELOW: Red Post Hill: the Casino Estate before development. The spire of the Herne Hill Congregational church is visible through the trees. The lake in the foreground which was surrounded by the grounds of Casino is now enclosed by Sunray Gardens. The Red Post Hill Land Company, a City-based developer, commenced building on this area in 1894.

OPPOSITE:House construction in the Oglander Road/Coplestone Road area of East Dulwich. ABOVE: Building begins. CENTRE: Ornate porches and bays embellish these houses. BELOW: Completed houses being moved into, in Oglander Road. Building began in 1879 and these higher rented houses had elaborate gables and other decorated features. Newly planted trees line the street. In the peak building years 1878-80, half the builders of East Dulwich erected only 1-6 houses. Only 20% built between 7-12 houses and a tiny proportion (3.6%) built more than 60 houses. ABOVE: Railway construction: the railways were responsible for the growth of Dulwich. The High Level line from Victoria to the Crystal Palace was opened in 1863 as a result of competition between the railway companies and transported millions to the front of the Palace. Six sets of tracks were at the terminus and an underground passage, faced with tiles and supported by cathedral-like columns linked the Palace to the terminus. BELOW: Lordship Lane Station.

OPPOSITE ABOVE: View of train from Cox's Walk bridge towards Lordship Lane station. The same view was painted by Pissaro and is hanging in the National Gallery. CENTRE: The bridge over the High Level line at Cox's Walk, now the Sydenham Hill nature reserve. BELOW: Train standing on the 'down' platform at Sydenham Hill station. ABOVE: The Cherry Tree, Grove Vale — Victorian public house respectability and a plethora of flowers. BELOW: Goose Green and St John's Church. The Green was once part of Peckham Rye Common. By the early 19th century it had a number of large houses with extensive gardens bounding it on the southern and western sides.

ABOVE: *Lordship Lane, at Goose Green. The East Dulwich Hotel on the left was the headquarters of the East Dulwich Cycling Club who held dinners and smoking concerts there.*

36 BELOW: *Shops in Lordship Lane at the corner of Hansler Road. The grocer's shop offers tea at 1/6 a lb.*

ABOVE: A horse 'bus passes the Magdala public house in Lordship Lane. BELOW: Lordship Lane — shops between Crystal Palace Road and Landells Road. INSET: The Dulwich Drug Store, the Dulwich Steam Laundry and Sayers' stand next to St Anthony's Hall, then a school.

ABOVE: A tram passes the horse 'bus terminus at the Plough, an advertisement for the New Cross Empire Music Hall on the side of the pub. BELOW: Mr Pay's grocer's shop and the row of old timber cottages opposite Dulwich Library, Lordship Lane. The spire of Emmanuel Church is just visible on the left.

ABOVE: Old houses in Lordship Lane, the spire of Emmanuel Church, Barry Road, in the distance. BELOW: Lordship Lane, looking towards St Peter's.

ABOVE: A tram passing the Grove Hotel, so named after the house on the site, used by Dr W. Glennie as a private academy. The young Lord Byron was a pupil. In 1888, the centenary of the birth of the poet, the Grove's owner placed a bust of Byron, with a laurel wreath, in the bar. BELOW: Looking down towards St Peter's from the railway bridge, Lordship Lane.

ABOVE: Dulwich Wood House, Sydenham Hill. BELOW: Houses in Underhill Road, with a change of style on the right, signifying a different speculative builder.

41

THE COLLEGE & 'THE BATTLE'

At the beginning of the Victorian era, the College of God's Gift, popularly called Dulwich College, was in a chaotic state. It had been founded in the early 17th century by Edward Alleyn, an Elizabethan actor who, to endow his foundation, had purchased the manor of Dulwich, an estate of almost 1,500 acres. Its value increased substantially when, from 1808, building leases of up to eighty-four years were granted. The annual surplus of income over expenditure was divided up among the College Fellows, and even the six poor brothers and six poor sisters had a portion. The Fellows rarely exerted themselves to teach any local children, as they were obliged to by statute. Indeed, they made a poor effort in teaching the twelve foundation boys, and consequently the College came under the scrutiny of the Charity Commissioners. At its first enquiry in 1833, the Commissioners discovered that more local children did not go to the College because their parents preferred to send them to the Dulwich Free School, which stood just a few yards from the College gates.

Four other parties had an interest in the College's wealth; these were the parishes which had been mentioned as beneficiaries in the Will of the Founder. Two of these, St Botolph's, Bishopsgate, the parish where Alleyn was baptised, and St Luke's, Finsbury, where he had his Fortune Theatre in Golden Lane, in the 19th century, were crowded, unhealthy City parishes. St Saviour's, Southwark, where Alleyn had his Bearpit and St Giles, Camberwell, his new parish, were also crammed with the poor, who the churchwardens felt should benefit from Dulwich's increased wealth, as Alleyn had envisaged.

The Charity Commissioners' case, brought by the Attorney General on behalf of these four parishes against the College, was heard in 1840-1 by Lord Langdale, Master of the Rolls. His Lordship found for the College; the parishes' claim was dismissed because Alleyn was not legally entitled to extend his charity beyond the terms of the Letters Patent he was granted in 1619, even though he clearly wished to do so in his will of 1626. Lord Langdale had a quiet word with the College's Master and it would seem that he advised him to devote some of the College's income to the provision of education for local children.

The College took this advice to heart; unquestionably Lord Langdale had also dwelt on the possibility of a total reform of the Charity if they failed to heed his warning. This of course was to happen sixteen years later. The College instructed its surveyor, Charles Barry (later knighted for his building of the Houses of Parliament), to erect the Grammar School, which opened in 1842.

A wide curriculum was offered by the new school, which was segregated into upper and lower divisions. The high standard set by the Grammar School's upper division provoked considerable envy among the foundation boys across the road at the College, who considered their education compared only with the 3d a week lower division, which indeed it did. The life of the Grammar School was short, a mere fifteen years, but it provided the sound base from which the new Dulwich College was launched, following the dissolution of the old foundation by Act of Parliament in 1857.

The College had not heeded any of the warnings it had been given and, with the popular outcry for the reform of corrupt charities, it was no surprise that, following a visitation by the Inspector of the Charity Commissioners in 1854, the end soon came. It had totally failed its pupils, none had gone on to university after 1771, and it was apprenticing boys to inferior trades instead of ones more appropriate to the higher education the boys were supposed to have received. One source revealed that neither of the teaching Fellows appeared in the schoolroom until 9.00 am, although the school officially started at 6.00 am, and that, if any boy was required to say a lesson as the result of only three hours' daily study, it was to a master, who heard it while remaining in bed! The Inquiry discovered that the two schoolmasters took it in turns to teach alternate weeks, and each blamed the different ages and capabilities of the twelve boys as the reason for their lack of progress. Both had totally ignored the Archbishop of Canterbury's injunction made only a few years earlier, to widen the curriculum by teaching the 15-16-year-olds surveying, chemistry and civil engineering. Apparently they found it easier to bring in part-time teachers to instruct the boys in French and drawing.

The Master, Warden and Fellows were all pensioned off — 'an expensive business', was the comment of Rev William Rogers, one of the new Governors appointed by Parliament. Rogers was the choice of Prince Albert, the Prince Consort, who had been impressed by his down-to-earth methods of providing education in the poorest parts of the City of London. He was also curate of one of the College's Foundation parishes and is remembered as the author of the famous quotation, 'Hang economy, hang theology, let us begin!' when addressing a gathering called to put up money for building yet another of his schools. With his appointment to Dulwich, he saw the opportunity to fill what he perceived as a gap in the provision of education,that of second grade schools for the expanding middle class. The poor were by now being reasonably well provided for, and the upper classes, wishing a classical education for their sons, could send them to one of the Great Schools.

The Government had invited Lord Stanley (later Earl of Derby) to be the first Chairman of Governors and the Board's choice of the new Master of Dulwich was Rev Alfred Carver MA, who had been under-master at St Paul's. Carver brought with him a classical background and the experience of administering a great public school, and he at once set about establishing the new Upper School as a first grade institution. One of the twenty boys transferred from the now dissolved Grammar School recalled how Carver immediately emphasised the importance of classics: 'Step forward any boy who knows any Greek'! For the boys themselves the shock of the new was in reality not too dissimilar from the comfortable years with the mild Dr Cox at the Grammar School. They still went on bird-nesting and snake-hunting expeditions in Dulwich Woods during the lunch break, and stories are legion of the grass snakes escaping from desks during the afternoon. The Upper School occupied the old College's schoolroom and further rooms were converted as the roll rose towards 150, the maximum the buildings could accommodate. The lower division of the Grammar School had become the College's Lower School and numbering 90, occupied both classrooms in the little building at the corner of Gallery and Burbage Roads.

The games the boys played during their 'breaks' would be, with minor changes to rules, still familiar to their modern counterparts. Marbles were the favourite, but Prisoners' Base and English and French were also popular. This last is interesting, as apparently in 1858 the French were still looked upon as the traditional enemy, despite the fact they had been allies in the recent Crimean War.

Two shops in the village were frequented by the boys; one was Lassam's the bakers (now the Post Office), which was famous for its jumbles at four for a penny, and ginger beer at twopence, but high class! The other favourite haunt was a sweet shop which stood almost at the school gates. For the boys of the Upper School, later to be officially called Dulwich College, there was the legendary Charlie Parsons, who was employed by the College as a gardener-cum-cleaner but who, with the Master's blessing, operated a tuck shop. Charlie's 'emporium' was improvised from a disused harness room in the yard, beneath the windows of the sixth form classroom. Here he dispensed apples, fly cakes, pear drops, sweet and sticky substances of all kinds, mostly for cash but sometimes for credit, a record of which was chalked up on the cupboard door.

Among the boys were a number of boarders, who resided at some of the large houses along the Village High Street. One of the boys boarding at Miss Field's got friendly with one of the Dudman family of blacksmiths, and persuaded him to teach him how to solder. With his new-found skill he manufactured rather crude but effective tinplate saucepans, which he sold for sixpence to his fellow boarders to boil chestnuts in.

The boys played football (rugby, not soccer) in the field which still exists beyond the Picture Gallery. They were often allowed to play cricket on the rather grand 'Gentlemen of Dulwich's ground' behind the Greyhound. Although overarm bowling was making its debut at the time, it was considered by the boys to be rather unfair and 'lobs' were held to be more sporting!

The Governors' shortage of sufficient funds to build the much-needed new college was solved when, between 1860-3, the London, Brighton and South Coast Railway and the London, Chatham and Dover Railway companies agreed to pay £1,000 per acre for the 100 acres of Dulwich they required for their tracks. This sudden windfall appears to have dazzled Rogers, who had spent most of his life scraping resources together to build schools. By now, he had been elected permanent Chairman, and he evidently carried the Board with him as Charles Barry Junior, who had succeeded his eminent father as surveyor, was commissioned to produce a design 'worthy of our aspirations and resources'. This Barry did; the result was Dulwich College, magnificent possibly, extravagant certainly. Its critics pointed out that, whereas the average cost of school building was £40 per pupil, Dulwich College cost £150 per pupil. The final costs were far in excess of the initial estimates and almost at once the Governors found themselves in financial difficulties again.

One of their options was to increase fees to generate more income. The storm this caused was to be eclipsed by those to come, but the opening salvoes of what became known as 'The Battle of Dulwich' were thus fired. The combatants in the 'battle', which lasted thirteen years, sometimes changed sides. Initially there was outrage that fees were being raised, when it was claimed that the wealth of the estate should enable them to be lowered, and the Governors were accused of making the new College accessible only to the rich. While there was some truth in these complaints, the actual number entering the school increased dramatically; Carver was relieved his dream of establishing a great public school could still be realised, and the Governors delighted they had confounded their critics.

Another cash-raising option pursued by the Governors was to sell building leases on the estate, under the supervision of Charles Barry. An advertisement in *The Builder*, inserted by him, guaranteeing a place at the new College for those who bought a building plot, caused further uproar, and the Governors' critics formed the Dulwich Education Committee, accusing the Governors of lowering standards by dispensing with the entrance examination.

The new College was officially opened in 1870 by the Prince of Wales, although it had been partially in use for twelve months. The success of the Upper School caused Carver to use the block originally designed to house the Lower School to accommodate the numbers seeking a place. The new College grew in numbers and reputation. Much was due to Carver's insistence on high academic standards, but also because he was supporting boys going on to university out of his pocket.

The Governors had not, however, abandoned their intention of making Dulwich a second grade school, and in the fourth of a series of schemes proposed by the Charity Commissioners, Dulwich was to be starved of cash in order that schools could be established in the two north Thames parishes, at a cost of £100,000 raised from the Dulwich estate. Two headmasters would run the Upper School, one in charge of the Classical side, the other, the Modern side. Further, it was proposed that the Lower School should be closed.

In 1876, with the publication of this scheme, the future of both Upper and Lower Schools hung in the balance. Carver appealed to the Privy Council, claiming that the new scheme would prejudice his salary and pension. The Privy Council found in his favour and the scheme was withdrawn. Carver's supporters recognised he had used the question of his emoluments only to smash the scheme and save the College, and they continued their opposition to the Governors who, with each succeeding scheme, conceded more ground. Finally, in the seventh scheme, published in 1881, and which passed through Parliament in the following year, the College received a substantial annual share of the estate's income, so enabling it to fulfil Carver's vision of a first grade public school in South London. The Act of 1882 also preserved the Lower School and ordered that new buildings should be provided, and that in future it should be called Alleyn's School.

The success of Dulwich College was therefore a result of the achievement of both Alfred Carver's and William Rogers' quite opposite aims. This combination of a public school in magnificent buildings naturally appealed to the rising middle classes of Victorian South London. They got the type of school they wanted and its success was unstoppable.

ALLEYN'S LEGACY

ABOVE: Dulwich College in 1840. Note the horse-drawn omnibus. OPPOSITE ABOVE: Tuition at the College: 'Neither of the teaching Fellows appeared in the schoolroom until 9.00 a.m. although the school officially opened at 6.00 a.m. and that if any boy was required to say a lesson it was to a master who heard it whilst remaining in bed!' BELOW: The Fountain and the Grammar School. This little building was built by Charles Barry in 1842. After the Act of Parliament of 1857 the former Grammar School was used by the boys of the Lower School, later Alleyn's School, until 1886. It then became the Village reading room.

47

ABOVE: The last Foundation scholars 1883, outside the Old College. Back row, left to right: Barker , the famous Charlie Parsons, (Beadle), Ransome, Payne and Herbert, centre; Spencer and Knight; front: Rev J. H. Smith (Headmaster) and standing behind him Stephenson, Ball, Foulds, Bosher and Gale. LEFT: Charlie Parson's tuck shop beneath the windows of the VIth form classroom. RIGHT: Tins of biscuits and jars of sweets line the shelves of the College's new tuck shop.

ABOVE: Dulwich College, known as the New College, opened by the Prince of Wales in 1870. BELOW: Dulwich College from the playing fields. The instant success of the New College persuaded the Master, Rev Alfred Carver, to change his plan of making the north block (left) the premises of the Lower School; instead the whole three blocks became Dulwich College.

49

OPPOSITE ABOVE: The science block and baths at the College, an addition to the original buildings and destroyed during World War II. BELOW: Concentration in the Classical VIth form. ABOVE: Alleyn's School 1893; senior boys pose on the school steps with their headmaster, Rev J. H. Smith, (right).

OTHER SCHOOLS

Apart from the College, Dulwich was also served by the Dulwich Free School and a number of private academies and dame schools. These were usually small, accommodating only a dozen or so pupils, often of both sexes, and of varying ages. They were principally for boarders, but were likely to have accepted pupils from Dulwich's middle class inhabitants.

The Free School had been founded by James Allen, the Master of the College in 1741, to provide elementary education for local poor boys and girls. He had endowed it with property in Kensington which, by 1814, had increased in rental sufficiently to improve and enlarge the school, and its roll soon reached 150. By 1830 an infants' class had been added, probably through the efforts of Mary Ranken, a local resident.

Miss Ranken continued to look after the running of the infant class until 1858, seeing to the purchase of books and materials and supporting it by collecting voluntary subscriptions for its maintenance. The Free School was restricted to girls and infants after the opening of the Grammar School, the boys entering the Lower Division. In 1857 a further change took place, when the Charity Commissioners separated the girls' and the infants' departments and, after some delay, the College built a new school for the girls' department further down the Village High Street.

Dulwich Girls' School, as it was now called, still offered the primary education it had always given but, by the 1870s, those parents whose sons were receiving a public school education at Dulwich College wanted a similar education for their daughters. Canon Carver, who was one of the three Governors of the Girls' School, was behind pressure on the Charity Commissioners to rethink their earlier ideas of establishing a higher-class girls' school in Camberwell. The Charity Commissioners agreed, and it was determined that the James Allen foundation should support a first grade girls' school in Dulwich.

Accordingly, in October 1886, James Allen's Girls' School was opened in East Dulwich Grove.

During those years local parents were concerned about the unsatisfactory condition of the infants' class, still situated in the Free School. A public subscription was launched to raise funds to provide a new infants' school to accommodate 150 children and, in 1865, under the aegis of the National Society, Dulwich Village Infants opened in its new building next to the Dulwich Girls' School.

In East Dulwich in June 1839 Rev Anderson, Minister of the Chapel-of-Ease at Goose Green, applied to the National Society for financial aid to build two schoolrooms for 75 boys and 75 girls. He wrote that he did not know how many persons the district comprised as there was no separate census taken for East Dulwich, but he guessed it was about 3,000. No schools existed there at all. A month later he was able to write to the National Society:

'It is with the greatest pleasure both on my own account and on that of the Society that I now beg leave to withdraw that application. I assembled a large party of my friends on Wednesday last at dinner in the Collegiate schoolroom at Camberwell and before we departed the whole amount was subscribed upwards of £500.'

East Dulwich's rapid development led to the school having to move to larger premises on the present site in North Cross Road in 1871. The children were expected to pay 1d-2d per week and this money was placed in a fund to clothe the poorer pupils.

The passing of the Education Act of 1870 provided for the formation of school boards with elected members. For the first time, women were allowed to stand for an elected post. The boards were required to build schools where there was an insufficiency, in order to provide elementary education for all children.

The London School Board gave notice of erecting a temporary iron building for Dulwich Hamlet (Boys) in 1883 and the school officially opened in February 1884 with a roll of 40. Plans for a permanent school for 240 were announced. The girls became part of Dulwich Hamlet School in 1886, after the move of James Allen's Girls' School to its new premises. So that the children might not be dispersed, the Board hired the vacated buildings. About half the girls transferred to James Allen's, the remainder became Dulwich Hamlet (Girls). The girls' department followed the usual pattern of expansion by the use of temporary iron buildings and, in 1893, 118 more girls were admitted. This number further increased, and permanent buildings to accommodate 358 girls were opened in 1897.

The ubiquitous iron buildings were frequently retained by schools for other purposes when new buildings were completed. The iron buildings at Dulwich Hamlet became manual training workshops and classrooms for what was at first entitled 'the continuation school'. This 'school' enabled pupils who left full-time education at 13 to return in the evenings, and for two shillings per term learn building construction, wood carving and machine drawing.

The girls' school buildings were reorganised in 1896 and now provided cookery and laundry centres, and a few years later two adjacent empty rooms in the old JAGS building were fitted up as a bedroom and sitting room, so providing a complete housewifery centre.

Attendance in the early years was sometimes erratic and absence usually coincided with some big event at the Crystal Palace. The Police Fête caused the school to close early in 1886, and a few years later all departments gave up any thought of opening at all on the day of the Fête.

The headmaster of the Hamlet, Mr C. Hunt, was in a similar mould to Canon Carver. He was ambitious for his school, even to the point where the Education Department considered he was running an elementary school on secondary school lines. His success, however, was considerable, and laid the foundation for the school's high tradition. In 1905 the Hamlet was asked by the London County Council to prepare an exhibition of drawings to be sent to Austria-Hungary, so that they could see the artwork done in elementary schools in London. French appeared on the curriculum.

The girls became proficient enough in drill to win the drill banner, the normal timetable being set aside to allow extra time for practice. In the boys' department, football became the life-blood of the school and was to lead to the formation of the later famous, Dulwich Hamlet FC. The twenty-first birthday of the girls' department was celebrated by a day out to the Crystal Palace 'and all were made happy with a tea and capital entertainment during the evening'. The boys had an outing to Box Hill, where a ramble was made and a cricket match followed. The day continued with tea at a farm, followed by the return walk to Leatherhead to catch the train home to Tulse Hill.

Class sizes in Dulwich schools were large, some rising to as many as 100 in the infants' department and 80 for the older children. In 1908 the LCC restricted class sizes to a maximum of 60, and in the same year finally put into effect the Employment of Childrens Act, passed five years earlier, which prohibited the employment of children under 11 and the part-time employment of schoolchildren before 6.00 am and after 8.30 pm.

Evening classes replaced the continuation class, but the aims remained the same — to offer continued education, to allow elementary educated children an opportunity for self-improvement. Shorthand, book-keeping, home-nursing and first aid were offered, and a study of the work of Shakespeare also appeared on the curriculum. Girls who had left school at 13 could come back in the evenings for gymnastics, callisthenics, indoor clubs and Highland dancing. Displays were frequently given. It compensated for their exclusion from such male-dominated clubs as the St Barnabas Institute.

In East Dulwich the LSB opened a temporary school in Heber Road in 1879 with a projected roll of 500, but by 1881 the amount of housing construction in the area required this to be doubled. However, families did not move into the completed houses as quickly as anticipated, and this number was not reached for another 20 years.

Goodrich Road School followed in 1886 and provided similar facilities to those of Dulwich Hamlet. Friday afternoons were set aside for organised play and games. Tennis, bagatelle, shuttles, draughts were listed. For the non-competitive, an opportunity was given to set out tea and dinner things or take a turn in a spelling bee.

Friern Road School (now Waverley School), which started life in a series of iron buildings in 1893, was in 1897 allowed to conduct experiments on instruction in domestic economy and cookery, in a centre specially set aside from the school itself. Children from other Board schools went to Friern for one afternoon per week, learning physics, chemistry, physiology and the chemistry of food.

In 1900 a meeting was held at St John's School, to inaugurate the opening of science and art classes in connection with the educational departments at Kensington, 'for the benefit of the inhabitants of East Dulwich and vicinity'. This was promoted, because a race was perceived for greater knowledge of scientific and technical subjects. It was feared that the Germans were elbowing out native young Englishmen in their own capital city. The Chairman of the meeting, Rev Dr Warburton, Vicar of St John's, considered the Germans were not only better linguists, but received a better technical education. America was also feared as a competitor. The Vicar did concede that progress had been made in England in the previous 10-15 years, and he noted that in some trades in London, French designers were employed, but these were now being replaced by English draughtsmen.

Private schools abounded in Dulwich in the second half of the 19th century; some only blossomed briefly. Some such as Oakfield and Dulwich Prep endured. Another was the Dulwich High School for Girls (now the home of Rosemead School), which was funded by the Girls' Public Day School Company in 1878 and which, under the capable hand of its first headmistress, Miss Ager, rose from an initial 40 girls to 820 by the end of the century. Dulwich College Preparatory School came into being when Dr Weldon, Carver's successor as Master of the College, took up his appointment in 1883. He found that the only prep school in addition to the College's own, was 'Miss Shorter's', a dame school run by two sisters in a house in Alleyn Park (then called Victoria Road). The Master invited J. H. Mason to start a school and allowed it to be called Dulwich College Preparatory School, but to be run entirely independently of the Governors. Accordingly, Mason started the school in a house just opposite the Alleyn's Head with 13 small boys in 1885. When Mason left two years later, the new Master, A. H. Gilkes, continued this mysterious patronage, and even appointed a successor in Rev J. H. Mallinson, who transferred the school to its present site in 1888. By the turn of the century there were 225 boys on the roll.

Denmark Hill School, housewifery in 1908. Domestic science or home economics became part of Dulwich's Board Schools' curriculum from 1897.

ABOVE: Dulwich Hamlet School. BELOW: Dulwich Hamlet School (Girls) domestic class 1907 in the 'sitting room'. Two rooms, previously the old classrooms of Dulwich Girls' School, were converted into cookery and laundry centres, and two fitted up as a bedroom and a sitting room.

OPPOSITE ABOVE: Dulwich Hamlet School (Boys) Headmaster, C. T. Hunt, in the school hall 1904. The Honours Boards were provided for boys to 'look up to' and recorded the names of those obtaining scholarships to local secondary grammar schools. 'The hall was small, intimate. Sitting at a raised desk was a plump man with full jowls and iron-grey hair. Father put his arm around my shoulders and propelled me forward, saying to the Headmaster that he wanted to enrol his son.' (Richard Church Over the Bridge). *BELOW: A practical botany class at James Allen's Girls' School in 1904, working on the natural order beds. Classes in the practical approach to botany were commenced at the school by Dr Lilian Clarke in 1896 and examples of native British habitat were reconstructed in the grounds. A salt marsh, a pebble beach, a country lane, a heath and a wood were all made. ABOVE: James Allen's Girls' School Sports 1890s.*

59

ABOVE: Friern School, 5th Standard science class, 1906.
BELOW: Goodrich Road School, manual work, 1906.

ABOVE: Goodrich Road School boys' rug-making, 1906.
BELOW: Friern Road School, drawing from models, 1907.

ABOVE: Goodrich Road School, Swedish drill, 1906. BELOW: Goodrich Road School, laundry class, 1906.

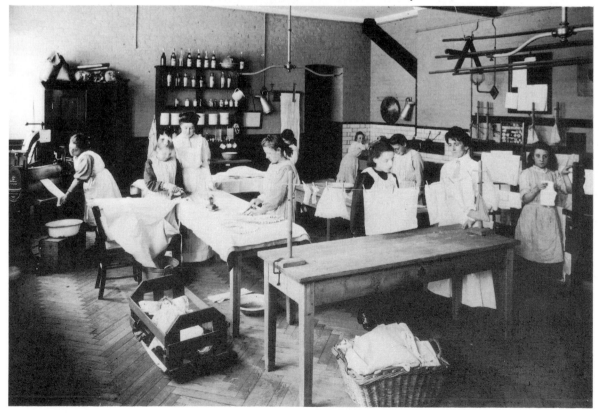

ABOVE: Goodrich Road School, nature class, 1906. Class numbers were as high as 80, reaching even 100 in some infants' departments. The LCC was to limit class sizes to 60 in 1908. BELOW: Physically handicapped children arriving by ambulance at Friern Road School, 1908.

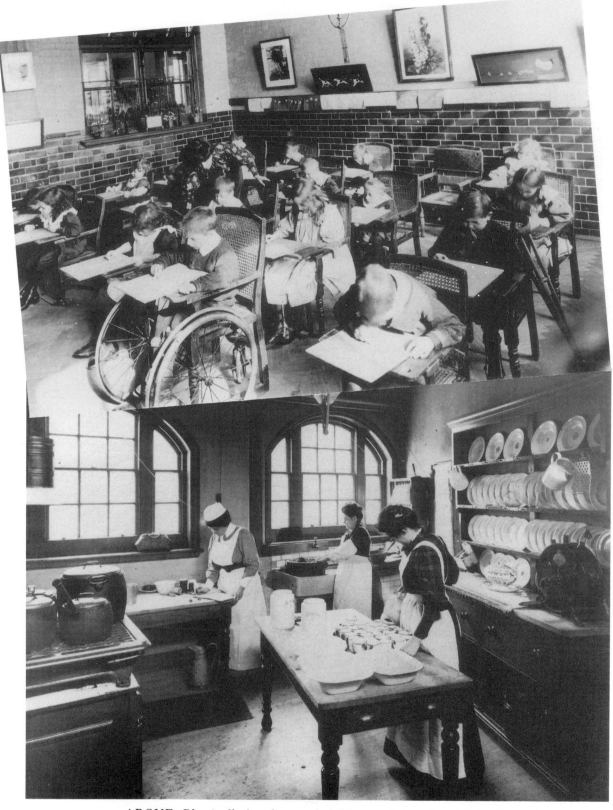

ABOVE: Physically handicapped children at Friern Road School.
BELOW: School lunches being prepared for the physically handicapped at Friern Road School.

*Children from Goodrich Road School having a practical nature
lesson at Peckham Park 1906.*

INNS & TAVERNS

Public houses in Dulwich were used for much more than the sale of alcoholic beverages in the Victorian period. Many were a focal point for social and business activities, and the use of some as a headquarters of local builders led to them being hired as venues for the auction of local land. Such sales were frequently held at the Grove Tavern.

At the Plough, Lordship Lane, long used as a terminus for horse buses, several lively and packed meetings took place in the late 1870s concerning the nuisance caused by gypsies, on vacant land at the Lordship Lane end of Friern Road. Large numbers were camping on British Land Company land, apparently with the Company's blessing. Complaints were made of petty larcenies, and damage to hedges and gardens caused by stray horses and donkeys. During 1878, 260 horses, 43 donkeys and six goats were taken to the pound by the police!

The new young Vicar of St Peter's, Rev Calvert, found himself in a difficult position; while he sympathised with residents who were having trouble with the gypsies as neighbours, he felt reluctant to side with them, as he felt it might make the gypsies think he was their enemy because they were poor and despised. He therefore left it in the hands of those who had called the protest meeting, who could 'act with greater freedom and with less serious risk than what I can do.'

The Chairman complained bitterly about the gypsies: 'Let the clergyman come and see the revelry and horse-racing which took place on Sunday, the eleven or twelve men he had seen stripped and fighting on a Sunday; let him, at 2 o'clock some mornings, come and listen to their making the night hideous. Let him see and hear these things and then let him try and convert them to another and a better life'. (Cheers)!! The Inspector of Nuisances had also visited the encampment, where he discovered a tribe of about 200. The continuance of the nuisance had paralysed fresh building or the attempt to sell completed houses. The Inspector reported that he had visited tents but, due to the fact that they kept large and fierce-looking dogs, it was dangerous to approach too near!

The Greyhound was more than a village inn, it was an institution. It had long been established and its grounds were extensive — two cricket fields, a bowling green and a menagerie. It provided splendid teas, and Ruskin, at the end of a day's sketching class with a group from J. D. Maurice's Working Men's College, would finish the day there. It shared with the Half Moon at Herne Hill a fame for its flowerbeds, but it was for its club room that it was also justly famous. It occasionally accommodated the Camberwell Vestry meeting for their deliberations, catered for club dinners and beanfeasts, and was the setting for most local celebrations. Notable of these was the quarterly meeting of The Dulwich Club, which celebrated its centenary in 1872. To the inn came the literary giants of Victorian society — Dickens, Browning, Thackeray and Mark Lemon, *Punch*'s first editor.

During this remarkable period the innkeeper was William Middlecott, a widower, who was assisted by his two daughters, a sister who acted as housekeeper, Sarah the barmaid, Susan the maid, and Catherine, the Irish cook. William Farmer from Oxfordshire was the potboy. Looking after the stabling for 15 horses and six coaches was William Devenport. The Greyhound changed hands a number of times towards the end of its life, the long reign of the Middlecott family at last over. The Temperance movement was strong in the Village. The new St Barnabas Church fostered two adult and one junior temperance societies and there was a national groundswell against alcohol, especially among women. As early as 1869, 42,877 attended a mid-week Temperance League Rally at the Crystal Palace.

The use of public houses for meetings of all kinds slackened as new public halls appeared. Imperial Hall, Lordship Lane, Dulwich Hall, Hindman's Road and Shawbury Hall provided accommodation and most of the newly built churches in Dulwich also included a hall in their building plans.

AT THEIR LEISURE

Denmark Hill; on the right is the Fox under the Hill inn.

ABOVE: The Half Moon, Herne Hill, noted in the 19th century for its flower gardens, lawns and tea garden. Quoits, bowls and lawn billiards were offered for outdoor entertainment. Dinners and beanfeasts were offered to societies, clubs and firms inside. BELOW: The 'new' Half Moon.

*OPPOSITE ABOVE: The footpath to Dulwich from the rear of the
Half Moon in 1876 (from a water colour at the Minet Library).
BELOW: Green Lane (now Green Dale), the route taken for
centuries by inhabitants of the hamlet of Dulwich to their parish
church at Camberwell. ABOVE: Norwood Lane (now Norwood
Road) before, and BELOW: during redevelopment.*

ABOVE: Horse-drawn buses and horse-drawn trams competing at the Thurlow Arms, West Norwood. On the left is the entrance to Norwood cemetery, opened in 1836 and the final resting place for many notable local celebrities — Maxim, Bessemer and Spurgeon. BELOW: Hearse en route to Norwood Cemetery in 1890.

ABOVE: Dulwich Court Farm, for many years the home of Colonel Constable (his christian name, not rank) until his death in 1877. He stood 6' tall and wore a wide-brimmed beaver hat, a high shirt collar, no neckerchief and had a smock front. Three of his sons assisted on the farm, which was to become Dulwich Park, and at one time it leased fields on the Common and on the east side of Lordship Lane. BELOW: Sheep being driven down the High Street of Dulwich.

*ABOVE: Pond behind Pond Cottages, also called Herring's Farm
in the 19th century after the Herring family of farmers. BELOW:
Pond Cottages.*

74

ABOVE: Dulwich Common in 1878, probably from the back of The Grange, looking towards Dulwich Wood Farm (from a painting in the Minet Library). BELOW: Dulwich Wood Farm, on the edge of Dulwich Woods, at the top of Grange Lane.

ABOVE: Cows being driven up Occupation Road (now Grange Lane) towards Dulwich Wood Farm. The house on the right is The Grange. BELOW: French's Meadows, later called Bell Meadows, Gipsy Hill, c1900.

ABOVE: Old houses in Lordship Lane, between Barry Road and Friern Road, on land belonging to Friern Manor Farm. In 1853 the farm was one of the largest in the vicinity of London, covering 200 acres. It employed thirteen milkers for its herd of 200 cows, which were milked twice a day. The cow-sheds were gaslit, allowing the milking to be done early, and on sale in the streets at 5 am. The farm was acquired for development by the British Land Company in 1865. BELOW: The Toll-gate, Court Lane. Woodbine Cottage was the home of the turnpike or toll keeper, Mr Purdy. Both this gate and the one in College Road were leased to him. There was considerable pressure in the 1870s to remove this toll gate which was claimed to merely act as a check on the other gate and was blamed for making houses difficult to let across Lordship Lane.

The Toll-gate, College Road.

ABOVE AND OVERLEAF: Croxted Lane: this ancient lane marked the boundary between Camberwell and Lambeth parishes and was also the western boundary of the Dulwich Manor. It was a favourite walk of John Ruskin.

79

THE PEOPLE IN THEIR PLACES

The people who lived in Dulwich came from many social backgrounds and the majority were born elsewhere. Predominantly, they came from the southern counties, those with an agricultural background probably driven from their original homes by increased mechanisation on the land. Many became gardeners, filling the gap in the local market caused by the wealthier arrivals' desire for formal flowerbeds and shrubberies. The Victorians' passion for their gardens made their maintenance the second largest occupation in Dulwich. The first was domestic service. The opportunities open to daughters of the working class were few. The better-educated might teach; the nimble-fingered might become dressmakers, but most became servants.

The great majority of servants in Dulwich were not born there. They, too, had left their villages to seek employment in the prosperous towns, especially London. While the keeping of a large retinue of domestic staff today might appear extravagant or eccentric, in the 19th century it was the means of maintaining the structure of society, giving security, accommodation and a wage to the struggling poor classes. So, while the fact that George Young, a 40-year-old widower living on Dulwich Hill (Sunray Avenue area) with his three children all under the age of five, and keeping a living-in domestic staff of three men-servants and thirteen female servants, might appear ridiculous to modern eyes, he may well have saved some of the sixteen from starvation or the workhouse.

So who were the ordinary people living in Dulwich?

In 1851 at Wellington Place, a cluster of six, tiny, weather-boarded cottages now covered by the science laboratories of James Allen's Girls' School, were living with their families an ostler from Kent and three gardeners, one from Wiltshire, one from Cambridge and one from Surrey. There was also a journeyman bricklayer and an agricultural labourer, both born in Dulwich. The last, Thomas Goodall, his wife and seven children, squeezed into one of the tiny cottages. One of the children, a 12-year-old, was already earning his living, working on a local farm.

Many families took in lodgers to help them pay their rents — at Herring's Cottages on Dulwich Common, George Caid, a haybinder from Lingfield, and his wife, Sarah, had their unmarried daughter, Sarah, who was employed as a housemaid, living with them, together with Sarah's two-year-old daughter. There were two lodgers: Edward Burham, a conductor from Staffordshire and John Page, a labourer from Dorset. While it was usual for the skilled men such as Caid, who lived in larger cottages, to have lodgers, the labourers and gardeners had no rooms to spare and, to bring in a little extra money, their wives took in laundry.

Until the mid-1850s, Dulwich remained an insular and self-sufficient place. Certainly its middle-class merchants would have taken the 9 o'clock stage-coach to Town, or one of the increasing numbers of horse-drawn omnibuses, and the wealthier would have been driven by their own coachmen. Several coach drivers lived in the village; one was Benjamin Doo, a 32-year-old widower, bringing up his six-year-old daughter Mary Ann, and four-year-old Eliza. Ben lodged in Boxall Row at the home of Robert Woodzell. Mrs Woodzell would have looked after the girls until Ben remarried. After his second marriage, he continued to live in Dulwich, and still drove the Sydenham coach.

Five men earned their living making and repairing boots and shoes, and the two village forges provided work for a number of blacksmiths. Several members of the Dudman family were smiths, following in the footsteps of their father, Dick Dudman, a blacksmith from Liphook in Hampshire. Craftsmen of this type lived in the three rows of tenements in the centre of the village, Garden Row, along the line of the present Aysgarth Road, Lloyds Yard, now partially the premises of W. J. Mitchell & Co, and Boxall Row, now rebuilt as Boxall Road.

The middle-class families living on Herne Hill would have considered that less than four servants was quite below their station. These Herne Hill socialites were solicitors, merchants or minor manufacturers. Some, like John Ruskin's mother, were uncomfortable in the society to which they had moved through hard work and thrift. She, for one, lived in isolation from her neighbours and, only after a great deal of heart-searching, was John allowed to make friends with a boy from a house close by, and then only following an interchange of letters between their fathers.

An even more affluent society lived on Champion Hill. Here, Joseph Dowon, a timber merchant and a widower, was helped by his 22-year-old daughter Caroline to bring up his three younger children, who were all at school. His domestic household comprised a butler, footman, coachman, gardener, cook, two nurses, two housemaids, and a kitchenmaid, a total staff of ten. Close by, William Stone, a silk broker, was living at Casino, a grand old house which had also had Joseph Bonaparte, uncle of the Emperor, as a resident. Stone had been the MP for Portsmouth and was the local JP. He, too, had a butler, three ladies' maids, a cook and a kitchenmaid to look after him, and the numerous relations who also made their home at Casino. Similarly, Matthias Attwood, a banker, living at Dulwich Hill, with his brother, Benjamin, a glass merchant, maintained nine domestic staff.

From the 1870s, undoubtedly one of the favoured new areas was Crescent Wood Road. Here gathered a number of wealthy merchants engaged in trade with Russia, Asia and Australia. There was also a sprinkling of German residents.

Two familes with the name of Peek, probably brothers, kept large households. William Peek, living at Shelton, had a governess for his six children and seven domestic servants. Francis Peek, living at Roby, only three houses away, was a tea merchant, and had a governess and eight domestic servants to look after his family of four children. He was extremely generous to the Anglican Church, agreeing to pay for the building of St Clement's, Friern Road, if nine others were built out of Diocesan funds and other monies. He also apparently gave a great deal of money for the building of St Saviour's, Coplestone Road. Henry Simmons at Tyersall, which he called after the place in Yorkshire where he was born, was a prosperous East India Company merchant, who had spent a number of years in Singapore. He had a governess to look after his four children, assisted by a schoolroom maid, a butler, three housemaids, a 16-year-old pageboy and a coachman.

A number of manufacturers favoured fashionable Sydenham Hill; access to London was close at hand *via* the new high level line from Victoria to Crystal Palace, and the views over the Weald to the south, and London to the north, impressive. The grounds of these mansions were large, running down from Sydenham Hill to the new railway line. Grottoes and ruins were constructed in the shrubbery-filled gardens. Frank Braby, at Mount Henly, a zinc manufacturer, had 285 men working for him at his factories, and on the other side of the road Charles Lazenby, the pickle manufacturer, built his massive house, Castlebar. The Avenue, now Dulwich Wood Avenue, attracted numbers of merchants, civil servants and professionals who, if not in the same league as the residents on the top of the hill, were still solidly middle class. James Dawson, a bookseller, employed 84 men in his company, and even Martin Fentinn, an ivory turner, employed 26. Acacia Grove, newly built in 1871, on part of the Dulwich Manor House estate, offered small houses to those striving for at least an appearance of Victorian 'station' — a single maid! Here were found those 'in trade', the clerks, and the purveyors of less desirable merchandise such as tallow.

Around the corner in Ildersley Grove the houses were of a slightly higher social status. At No 12, one of Joseph Harris's developments, lived Judge Peterson with his wife Mary, their five children and a nurse, cook and housemaid.

The judge and his family would have wondered what noise they heard on 22 January, 1887. It was not, as one resident suggested, the beat of a drum of a new wing of the Salvation Army! It was H.M. Stanley testing a machine gun in the garden of Hiram Maxim's house around the corner at Thurlow Lodge. Stanley found the Maxim gun could fire 600 rounds a minute and, with a defensive shield, would be extremely useful for his relief column to rescue Emin Bey, hemmed in at Wadelai on the Nile. He left directly for Zanzibar with his new weapon.

In East Dulwich there were also some roads which were more 'desirable' than others. Whateley Road had a mixture of craftsmen and clerks living in houses of multiple occupancy. William Mote and his family, however, required all of their house. He was a 53-year-old solicitor's clerk, born in Clerkenwell, and his wife Martha used to be an artificial flower maker, no doubt for the millinery trade; the two older daughters aged 24 and 22, were dressmakers and the eldest son, William, aged 20, was a merchant tailor's assistant. Hurden, aged 18, worked in a greengrocery and 15-year-old Rebecca stayed at home helping mother. Three more children were at school, including the seven-year-old twins, Evangelina and John.

In Etherow Street there were signs of the forthcoming emancipation of women. Rebecca Read was a 38-year-old widow from Ireland, a fiction writer, supporting her three sons and a daughter, by her writing. Living with Rebecca was her mother, Margaret Fisher, who also earned her living, working as an accountant. Dwelling in the same house was another family, the Cartwrights. Percy was a young Law Stationers' printer, and his wife, Agnes, had a nine-month-old baby son. Percy must have had a good job, because he employed a domestic servant and a 15-year-old nursemaid to look after his family.

And then there was Underhill Road, its tall houses often accommodating three families. Here lived many of Camberwell's clerical population, representatives of a borough with the largest concentration of clerks in London, all helping to turn the mercantile wheels of London's trade with the world.

HANDSOME HOMES

Fashionable Herne Hill: architectural designs of early Victorian houses.

The Triangle, Denmark Hill, 1908.

85

*ABOVE: Gate at Champion Hill, erected by the residents'
association in the 1840s to 'keep the rabble out'! BELOW: John
Ruskin's house, Denmark Hill. 'The view from the breakfast room
into the field was really lovely. And we bought three cows, and
skimmed our own cream, and churned our own butter. And there
was a stable, and a farmyard, and a haystick and a pigstye and a
porter's lodge where undesirable visitors could be stopped before
startling us with a knock.'* Praeterita. *LEFT: John Ruskin's house
from the garden, c1905.*

ABOVE: Sir Henry Bessemer's house, Denmark Hill. Bessemer purchased the 40-acre estate in 1863, naming it Bessemer House. He divided his estate into six parts: a model farm, a small deer park, a large artificial lake, a series of caverns, hidden in which was a gilded room with mosaic ceiling and walls, and lawns and shrubberies. He lived at Bessemer House until his death in 1898.
BELOW: Bessemer House from the lake.

The Conservatory, Bessemer House, designed by Charles Barry.

OPPOSITE ABOVE: The drawing room, Bessemer House.
BELOW: Bessemer's Observatory adjoining Green Lane contained
the world's second largest telescope.

ABOVE: The Grange. This Elizabethan style house was built next door to Bessemer House and given by Bessemer as a wedding present to his daughter. BELOW: Fairfield, Dulwich Village.

ABOVE: The garden, Fairfield. Note the newly built tower of St Barnabas Church. BELOW: College Gardens, a Victorian development on the former gardens of the Old College.

OPPOSITE ABOVE: Eastlands, Court Lane, c1890, the home of Mr C. Higgins, a partner in the firm of Jones & Higgins of Peckham. The house had previously been used as a private academy by Rev Philip Butt, and afterwards by the Turkish Ambassador as a summer residence. BELOW: The garden, now covered by Eastlands Crescent. ABOVE: Lordship Lane at the corner of Court Lane. BELOW: Belair, Gallery Road, once the home of Mary Ranken, and later Sir Evan Spicer.

93

ABOVE: Victorian elegance and charm in the garden of The Grange, Grange Lane. LEFT: The Grange. RIGHT AND OPPOSITE ABOVE: Victorian decor inside. BELOW: The Manor House, Dulwich, demolished in 1880 for development.

ABOVE: The lake and terrace, Kingswood. BELOW: The once modest Georgian house, extended and clad in battlements by John L. Johnston, the inventor of Bovril, in 1892. The house was nicknamed 'Bovril Castle' by the villagers.

96

ABOVE: Prince Charles' room and bed from
Culloden House at Kingswood. The bed was slept
in two nights before the Battle of Culloden by
Prince Charles and for two nights after his defeat
by the Duke of Cumberland. BELOW: A
romantic 'ruin' created by Johnston at Kingswood.

ABOVE: The Hall, Kingswood, now the Kingswood Adult Library. LEFT: The Billiards Room, Kingswood. The mantlepiece was rescued from the Palace of St Cloud, before it was destroyed by the Prussians in 1870. The room is now the Junior Library. RIGHT: The Dining Room, Kingswood, now used as a Day Centre.

98

PLIGHT OF THE POOR

Just how did the poor manage for food, clothing, education, housing, health care, before the State ensured the population would have them by right? They usually obtained them by a combination of personal thrift and the acceptance of help from the better-off. Although the 1832 Poor Law had ensured that no one need starve in England, its rules were stringent. For the old and infirm poor, help was freely given, usually by the unfortunate person entering the workhouse or 'union', as it was more familiarly called. For the inhabitants of Dulwich this meant the parish workhouse in Havil Street, Camberwell, or Gordon Road, Peckham, when that opened in the 1870s. Local relieving officers were also able to issue a voucher exchangeable at local shops for bread but, for the long-term unemployed, there was no alternative to the union than starvation. Here husband was separated from wife, and children above nursing age from mothers. Children were sent to Sutton, where fresh air and schools were provided for them. Mostly they were orphans or illegitimate, abandoned by pauper parents, and it was considered that their removal from 'scenes of drunkenness, filth, disorder and violence, neglect of religious observances and practice of positive vices in which they have been reared . . .' was the Poor Law Commissioners' duty. Through the exertion of Dulwich's general practitioner, Dr George Webster, a convalescent home was purchased at Herne Bay for these children.

The Guardians of the Poor had little sympathy for the able-bodied poor. These, it was felt, were a burden on the rate-paying community, and so the workhouse was made as unpleasant as possible for such inmates. They were required to perform physical labour to offset part of the cost of their keep. Such men at Gordon Road Workhouse were required to break 5-7 cwt of granite per day into small pieces. In 1879, when this was found to be an insufficient task to occupy the men for the whole day, the weight was increased to 7-10 cwt and the pieces were to be small enough to pass through a 2″ mesh. In 1896 official attitudes hardened further and the size of the mesh was further reduced to 1½″.

Of course, many inhabitants took pity on the poor. Colonel Constable at Court Farm frequently let tramps sleep overnight in his barn. In 1851 on the day the census was taken, he had no less than five such 'guests'! The mentally subnormal were treated sympathetically, and the Camberwell Guardians maintained them in asylums. In 1884 there were 170 such cases in the parish of Camberwell. For the mentally handicapped who could fend for themselves, casual employment, usually in the form of gardening, was often offered.

For almost thirty years, until the death of her cousin Charles Ranken of Belair, in 1858, caused her to leave Dulwich, Mary Ranken organised a number of forms of social welfare among the poor of the village. Helping the poor was one of the few occupations considered 'respectable' for women. Mary press-ganged friends and relations into her enterprises, which later became known collectively as the

Dulwich Local Charities. These included a provident thrift club, whereby small savings could be made and interest earned, a boot club to provide shoes for the poor, a coal club, and a provident dispensary. She also organised subscriptions for the maintenance of the infants' class at the Free School and clothing for the children. In this way some twenty girls and twelve boys from the village were clothed. At the beginning of Victoria's reign it was also customary at Christmas for the better off to take presents to the poor of Dulwich.

Mary Ranken was not the only friend of the poor. An earlier benefactor had left money to provide bread and potatoes for twenty families in the hard winter months, and in 1865 Benjamin Attwood, who had been left a fortune by his nephew Matthias, a member of the wealthy banking family, gave an estimated £375,000 to various hospitals, infirmaries and dispensaries.

Another generous resident, living on fashionable Denmark Hill, was T. Lyon Bristowe, MP for Norwood. He gave a 'treat' to 500 children from poor families to which other local residents gave donations. The weather on that occasion was lovely 'and the children ate such pie, bread and butter and cake, milk and fruit as they could manage'. Mr Tapling at Kingswood frequently received cartloads of children for tea and games.

Children at the Board schools had no free school dinners by right but Free Dinner Committees raised money to ensure children benefited from at least one good meal a day. Dulwich's poor were not likely to have been quite as desperate as those of the Borough, Southwark, when as late as 1887 the headmaster of a school in the Mint wrote his thanks to his local committee, saying that several children were saved from absolute starvation by their efforts.

Similar committees were established to provide funds for boots for poor Board school children, just as Miss Ranken had done almost fifty years before the first Board school appeared in Dulwich. Concerts were given regularly for such good works. Before 1882 a small weekly fee was payable by Board school children. These were often applied to a fund to provide shoes and clothes for the poorer children.

Health care among the poor of the village was provided for through the provident dispensary or the sick club, to which families contributed a small weekly subscription. A similar scheme was started at St Peter's, Dulwich Common, in 1886 and another existed in West Dulwich, which was also supported by subscription from the better-off. The weekly payment was usually 2½d and intended for those whose weekly wage did not exceed 35s. Before Dulwich was served by main drainage in the middle of the century, there were frequent outbreaks of typhoid. As the incidence of these fell, diphtheria and scarlet fever replaced them as the greatest threats to health, especially to the young.

The services of a Queen's Nurse became available towards the end of the century, her attendance being paid for by subscription made at the College Chapel. During April and May 1893, nurse, Miss Moncrieff, made 723 visits in the parish of St Barnabas, some of her twenty-seven cases requiring several visits per day. By the end of May, ten cases remained on her books, eleven were convalescing, one had gone to hospital and three had died. Of the three who died, one was a girl suffering from peritonitis and one a boy suffering from phthisis.

During the Victorian and Edwardian period, there was no local hospital in Dulwich, although in 1894 a meeting was held to consider the need for one. Mr Hemans of Holland House, Lordship Lane, had offered the use of his premises, rent-free, for two years, but he required the lease to be purchased at the end of the period. The organisers of the meeting failed to receive sufficient promises of support to accept his offer. The poor of Dulwich were thus obliged to travel to Guy's or St Thomas's Hospitals, even if they had an accident, or were ill at night.

The large infirmary in East Dulwich Grove, belonging to the Southwark Union (now Dulwich Hospital), was opened in 1887, despite considerable local opposition led by such prominent residents as Sir Henry Bessemer, whose house looked down upon the proposed infirmary, and Charles Barry, the College's Surveyor, who was concerned that it might be a nuisance and injurious to the property in the neighbourhood. The Infirmary was built in Dulwich after a number of years of wavering. The Southwark Infirmary at Newington (Elephant & Castle) was overcrowded, and the healthy air of Dulwich was welcomed as beneficial to the sick. The Infirmary, which took two years to build, had 732 beds.

The poor and even the working class had a dread of ending their days in the workhouse, and it was a stigma which, for a time, was to hang over the future Dulwich Hospital, even when the workhouse system was abolished.

PUBLIC PLACES

ABOVE: Southwark Union Infirmary, East Dulwich Grove, c1905, later Dulwich Hospital. Opened in 1887 with twenty wards containing 26-30 beds and twenty-four two-bed isolation wards, it was built to take the overflow of pauper sick from Southwark workhouses. OPPOSITE: Female wards at Southwark Union Infirmary, with individual curtaining.

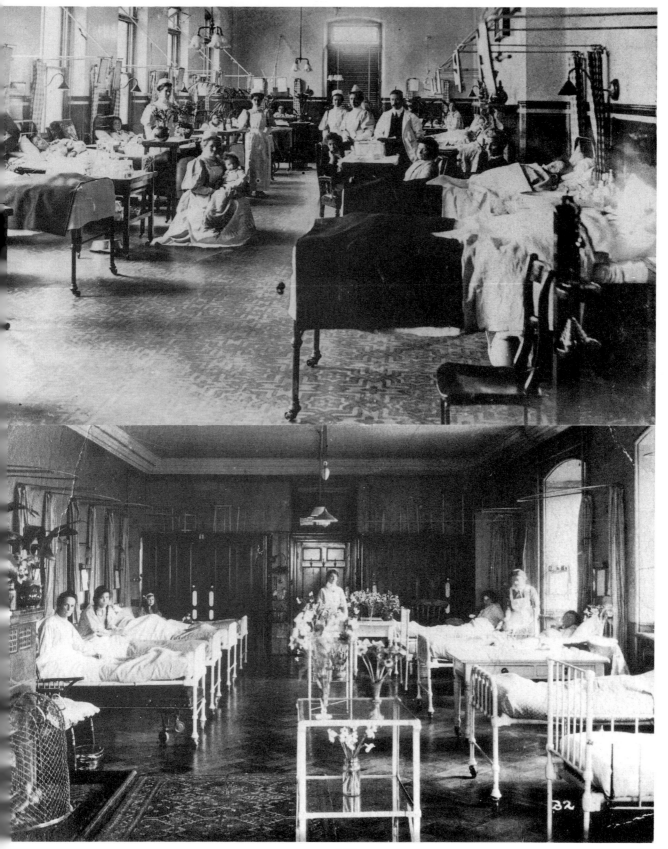

103

ABOVE: Gordon Road Workhouse, showing, LEFT: the 1½" grilles through which granite pieces had to pass after being crushed by the workhouse male inmates. Each man was required to break up 7-10cwt of granite per day. The daily diet for these men in 1895 was 8oz bread, a pint of gruel for both breakfast and supper, 2oz cheese and two meat dishes each week. RIGHT: East Dulwich Police Station, Crystal Palace Road, 1908. Rosebank had been purchased in 1882 by the Metropolitan Police as a station, after an approach by the house's owner, Mrs Taite. Two adjoining shops were also purchased. The lodging assessment for the resident married inspector was 5s 6d per week.

Dulwich Fire Station: the engine gallops from the station down Lordship Lane. The station was opened in 1893 and accommodated 10 firemen (all married men) and four horses. The appliances were a steamer, one manual engine and four fire escapes. It took 25 seconds from an alarm being raised to the departure of the appliance. The first call of the newly opened station was at 2.40 am following the opening, to a fire at St John's Villas, Goose Green.

105

ABOVE: Dulwich Park was amongst the last of the Victorian parks and although its layout has many features in common with earlier parks, by the 1890s fashions were changing. The highly coloured geometrical flower bedding schemes which once had been so popular were 'out' and 'in' were the less formal herbaceous borders and naturalised planting, a good example of which was BELOW: the American Garden, the later famous rhododendrons, photographed from the tower of the Fire Station. The Park was constructed at a cost of £35,000 on the former fields of Dulwich Court Farm, Bell Meadows and Rushton's Fields, land given by the Alleyn College Estates Governors. It was opened by Lord Roseberry in 1890. OPPOSITE: The carriage drive.

LEFT: The Aviary, Dulwich Park. RIGHT: The stone and rustic bridges. BELOW: Perambulators and perambulations in the Park.

ABOVE: The Lake, Dulwich Park. This feature was a great attraction from the beginning, but there was considerable opposition to the introduction of boats in 1906 when it was feared it might lead to rowdiness. BELOW: Brockwell Park, rustic bandstand and Brockwell Hall.

ABOVE: The clocktower, and BELOW: sheep keeping the grass short, both at Brockwell Park.

SPORT AND RECREATION

Early in the Victorian period hunting was a sport practised by many elements of Dulwich society. For the wealthy there was the opportunity to join the staghunt, which frequently assembled at the Beulah Spa. The Spa itself was a social centre. The stag was occasionally chased into Dulwich and one was caught in the yard of The Greyhound. The animal was removed in a boxcart and released on the following Saturday's hunt. On the next occasion he ran to Dulwich he made for the Millpond, where he swam across the water chased by the hounds. The stag was last seen making off, back in the direction of Croydon. Croydon was also the venue for a kangaroo hunt attended by some Dulwich residents which, while acclaimed a success, did in fact result in the kangaroo being released from a cart, taking to the hills and outjumping the field!

Dulwich Woods were still a popular hunting area, and the College employed George Ward as gamekeeper. The last College Warden, R. W. Allen, kept sporting dogs for the shooting season and hunted there with his steward and bailiff. Some of the village shopkeepers kept beagles for hunting hares and rabbits and on occasions they would also run a competition for the best dog. This started at the bottom of Court Lane, when a dead rabbit would be dragged on a length of string by a good runner. After 10-15 minutes the dogs would be released to follow the scent, on a course which took them over the Five and Fourteen Fields and finished on the Common. The first dog to arrive at the finish was awarded the rabbit. Fox hunting was conducted by the Surrey Hounds which, at one time, had their kennels at the foot of Dog Kennel Hill. Much of the sport was abandoned in 1845 on the introduction of a tax on keeping dogs.

A good deal of exchange visits took place among the Dulwich upper classes and on these occasions it was usual to entertain guests with some form of musical recital or play a rubber of whist after dinner. Garden cultivation was considered an acceptable diversion, and properly constituted Flower Societies existed at both ends of the social scale. In 1869 the Dulwich Flower Show was open to two classes of entrant — the professional gardener who was employed by the owners of Dulwich's grand houses, and the cottagers who lived in the Village or abutting Lordship Lane. It was quite an event, taking place in the Infants' and Dulwich Girls' Schools, where a musical background was provided outside by the 'P' Division Police Band.

In the upper classes, differences had arisen between two local horticultural societies — the Surrey and the New Surrey Floricultural Societies and, in 1870, a deputation from each waited upon Rev W. Powell, Vicar of St Paul's, Herne Hill, one November evening. The Surrey Floricultural had existed for over a quarter of a century and was made up of members of the local clergy and gentry of Brixton, Dulwich and Herne Hill. While it had been extremely successful, a dispute had broken out four years earlier and some members formed a breakaway society

111

named the New Surrey, thus beginning a great confusion to many local subscribers, who merely wished to encourage the growing of flowers. Both societies agreed to try to resolve their differences and the President of the New Surrey, Rev Ransford of All Souls, Dulwich Road, reached a 'peaceful settlement' with the President of the original society, Rev G. K. Flindt of St Matthew's, Denmark Hill. Rev Powell, who mediated was, it transpired, a vice-president of the new society!

For the working class, the working week was usually of six days, a half-day holiday being the subject of much debate from 1886. Bank holidays, therefore, were looked forward to most of all by the poorer inhabitants. For such as these, Peckham Rye acted as a strong magnet and, although the Metropolitan Board of Works took over the Rye in 1883, and laid out some of its barren ground with plants and shrubbery, the stalls of itinerant traders were still the greatest source of interest. The authority clamped down on some of these traders, but many found spots for their exhibitions of unnatural oddities. A steam-driven roundabout, shooting galleries and donkey rides all proved in popular demand, but the real craze in the 1880s was skipping!

For the better off, bank holiday meant either an excursion by train to the seaside or, more popularly, up the Thames by steamer to Margate. The wealthy had been taking this route to Margate for years and it was usual to spend anything up to five weeks of the summer at the resort.

The Crystal Palace was, of course, the greatest attraction, and on Easter Monday, 1883, it was host to no less than 61,115 visitors.

Recreation, as practised by the Victorians, was also cultural — the Herne Hill Working Men's Club presented an entertainment entitled *The Pickwickians at Dingley Dell* in 1869, and two years later the sister club in Dulwich published its 6th annual report, which commented on the satisfactory progress it had enjoyed under the Presidency of Dr Carver. It had recorded a good attendance in the reading room and the writer was grateful to be able to record that 'Mr John Ruskin takes an interest in the association to which he has presented a valuable collection of minerals and fossils'.

The Herne Hill and Dulwich Social Club was in existence in 1871 and met on Friday evenings at the Half Moon. The evening took the form of a 'sumptuous banquet prepared by Mr J. C. Coles, the worthy host of this ancient hostelry'. Such gathered were all male affairs, and the procedure of the evening invariably followed a similar pattern, of which this particular meeting is a good example. There was the 'removal of the cloth', which signalled that dining was done and entertainment would follow. This took the form of numerous speeches and toasts to the various officials, followed by, or interspered with, songs or recitations by some of the members. So the fifty assembled club members at the Half Moon that particular Friday heard Mr Lassam, the village baker, sing *Nil Desperandum* followed by Mr Copping singing *The Four Jolly Smiths*.

A more serious society was formed in 1899 — The Dulwich Scientific and Literary Association which, for 10s per annum, offered fortnightly lectures in winter and occasional excursions in summer. The Edwardians displayed an inclination towards Shakespeare, and a Shakespeare Society performed regularly at the Imperial Hall (later the site of the Odeon Cinema, Grove Vale). Its first production of the 1909 season was *Romeo and Juliet*.

112

The Benedict Musical Society, which presented its concerts at the Castle Hotel, Crystal Palace Road, had a most varied programme at its fourth concert. Mr Stuart Lane opened the proceedings with the overture from *Tancredi* and Mr Max Leog of the German Musical Society gave a 'truly artistic rendering of the favourite "Vicar's Song" from "The Sorcerer".'

A reading room had been established in the Village during the 1860s but when, in 1886, the Grammar School was vacated by Alleyn's School, the building was adapted as a new reading room. Although there was great public pressure locally for free libraries it still remained the responsibility of the wealthier classes to provide books for the intellectual improvement of the lower orders. It would be another ten years before the Camberwell public library village branch opened at the Reading Room, and this was largely through the generosity of Evan Spicer of Belair, who started it with a stock of 600 books.

With the taking over of most of the turnpikes in South London by the Vestries in 1865, and the gradual improvement in the roads, albeit they remained extremely muddy in bad weather, the sport of 'cycling became very popular.

The Dulwich Bicycle Club was formed in the Village and held its club dinners at the Greyhound. In 1887 medals were awarded to all members who rode 100 miles in 10 hours, no mean feat considering the state of the roads and the solid tyres with which the bicycles and tricycles were equipped. The Club also ran competitions for swimming and shooting and their runs started from the Fountain in the village.

The East Dulwich CC met at the East Dulwich Hotel, Goose Green, and its 'cycling runs usually boasted a dozen members. The last run of the season in October 1886 was to Sutton where, on arrival at the Cock Inn, dinner was followed by the traditional toasts, interspersed with songs. Although the report does not say so, presumably they all rode back again! The activities of the club did not close for the winter; at last the ladies were entertained, when six Cinderella dances were arranged.

For 'cyclists living in South Dulwich, their local society was the South Roads Club, which met at the White Hart assembly rooms. Although the Club had only been in existence for three months, by December 1886 its secretary, H. Grist, could proudly announce that it had gained 60 members and had carried out a road race.

The great popularity in 'cycling was not confined to men; it was also considered a proper exercise for women, but membership of local clubs was confined to males. In 1890 it was announced that a syndicate had purchased a large piece of ground to the north of the Greyhound as a new recreation ground for South London. It was to be laid out with a 'cycle track, with a pedestrian track inside. The 'cycle track was to have banking which, at the curve, would reach a height of nearly 6 feet. It is an indication of the popularity of the sport that the proximity of another track at the Crystal Palace did not deter the promoters. The complex was also to include a football field and six or more tennis courts.

Cricket was apparently the sole event in Dulwich in which all classes joined together for a common purpose. The principal cricket ground in Dulwich was behind the Greyhound, and the Dulwich Cricket Club included Dick Dudman, the local blacksmith, and Bob Redman, the demon bowler, over 6' tall and a local hero who had served in the Crimean War.

ON PLEASURE BENT

ABOVE: Dulwich Picture Gallery had been a long established favourite of the Victorians. It was considered an ideal venue to make up a party to visit. Frequent visitors included Robert Browning and the Prime Minister, W. E. Gladstone, and his family. BELOW: Mr Hodgkins, the curator and his friend.

ABOVE: Peckham Rye, The Bandstand, and BELOW: Bank Holiday crowds and the famous donkey rides.

The Horniman family at Surrey Mount 1891.
The museum sprang from the private collection
of Frederick Horniman, a tea merchant. He
opened it to the public at his home, but by 1896
the collection had outgrown the house and in
1901 his son Emslie masterminded the setting up
of the publicly-owned museum.

*ABOVE: The early days of the museum at
Surrey Mount. BELOW: The interior of the
'new' Horniman Museum. OPPOSITE
ABOVE: The opening ceremony of BELOW:
the Horniman Museum, the destination of
countless Edwardian families, designed by C.
Harrison Townsend.*

116

ABOVE: Herne Hill Stadium, early days. BELOW: Old Kennels, Dog Kennel Hill, home of the Surrey Hounds, dismantled 1908.

Children's fancy dress at INSET: Dulwich Baths.

Thomas Tilling horse 'buses ABOVE: at Jones & Higgins, Peckham and BELOW: awaiting departure. Tilling began his jobbing business with a single horse in Walworth in 1845, and in 1858 bought a single omnibus and started a service of four 'buses a day between Rye Lane and Oxford Circus at a fare of 1s 6d. Within 20 years his stable had grown to 400 horses and in 35 years to 1,500. On May Day 1871 he assembled 20 omnibuses in Peckham High Street and presented a perambulation of the district in its May blossom; the excursion was a huge success, even if the weather was chilly!

ABOVE: Outing from the Crystal Palace Tavern. BELOW: Baden-Powell Scouts at St Barnabas, Canon Nixon in the centre.

PARISH & PRAYER

The ancient parish boundaries of the church of St Giles, Camberwell, existed for much of the 19th century. The parish included Camberwell, Peckham, East Dulwich and the hamlet of Dulwich. The neighbouring, vast parish of Lambeth, had been partially broken up by the creating of new parishes at Brixton and Norwood early in the century.

Until the 1890s the hamlet of Dulwich remained so sparsely populated in comparison with the remainder of the parish that Christ's Chapel, which was built by Edward Alleyn in 1616, was adequate to cope with local needs. Some inhabitants, of course, made their way to the parish church of St Giles. Early in the century a chapel-of-ease was established at Goose Green, which was the precursor of the parish church of St John's, consecrated in 1865, the £8,000 required for its building being raised by public subscription. St Stephen's in College Road followed in 1868, the building of this church being a result of the Dulwich College Act of 1857, which required the College to fund the building and to establish an ecclesiastical district in South Dulwich. Because most of its congregation lived in large detached mansions, it had a small, but exclusive, electoral roll. The finery of the dress worn for church by the female members of the congregation gained for St Stephen's the nickname 'The Butterfly Ball Church' among inhabitants. In the Village the Chapel continued to serve the villagers' needs and the College Chaplain, Rev John Oldham, performed the duties of a vicar by taking over the management of the Dulwich Local Charities following the departure of Mary Ranken.

St Peter's, Dulwich Common, was erected in 1876 on land given by the College, but it had started its life several years earlier, in a temporary iron church on the other side of Lordship Lane. The non-conformist church was particularly strong in East Dulwich, where the Dulwich Grove Chapel, built to accommodate 300 worshippers in 1879, was required to be replaced by the present church, then holding 1,000, in 1890. The Baptists were numerous enough in the village for the headmistress of Dulwich Hamlet School (Girls) to note that a number of children were absent from school on account of Rev Charles Haddon Spurgeon's funeral.

The sequence of the building of St Barnabas was similar to that of a number of other churches. Firstly, a temporary iron church was erected at the corner of present-day Woodwarde Road in 1891 and the new young Vicar, Rev Howard Nixon, commenced the formidable task of establishing a congregation, only a few hundred yards from the College Chapel. There was, however, a significant difference between the two village churches, in that Nixon made every effort to bring the lower classes to his new church. He also provided facilities to attract local youth. This he did by promoting various sporting activities and linking his church with Dulwich Hamlet School. A gymnastic class was formed in the early 1890s and was run by Canon Daniel, Chaplain of the College. Daniel was to support the new church and worked closely and well with Nixon.

Nixon took over the management of the old Dulwich Local Charities in 1893 and added a Slate Club to the list. All working men were invited to join, and the subscription of sixpence a week entitled members to attend a club night social evening, as well as providing funeral aid and financial help to married men. It encouraged debate on contentious subjects such as 'Capital Versus Labour'. Nixon also reorganised the Coal Club and persuaded the villagers to form a co-operative to buy in bulk when the price of coal was low. Efforts were made to support the work of MABYS (Metropolitan Association for Befriending Young Servants), whose aim was to supply a friend for every young girl coming from home to enter service or work in London.

St Barnabas strongly promoted temperance and from 1899 ran a Band of Hope and a branch of the Church of England Temperance Society. The work was supported by A. H. Gilkes, Master of the College, who proposed that the closing of public houses should be preceded by the establishment of houses where men could go instead. Gilkes claimed that he did not think men resorted to public houses merely for the sake of drinking, but rather for companionship. Working men were often, owing to the wretched state of their homes, driven out of an evening.

Possibly as a result of this suggestion, the St Barnabas Institute was founded the following year. Existing activities, such as the gymnastic class, came under the new banner, which was expanded to include a cricket club which had started life as the St George's Institute CC in Colwell Road. A football team called Dulwich St Barnabas FC was also formed. Soon, a debating society was started by members of the Institute and its meetings on Saturday evening discussed such topics as vaccination, social reform, liberty of the press and women's rights. The debates often alternated with musical evenings, which provided a popular innovation. Tents were regularly used for the evening functions, when an audience of over 100 was usual. Membership of the Institute was, however, restricted to the young men of the parish.

The church had a thriving Sunday School and its annual fête was usually held in the field next to Eastlands in Court Lane, or at Dulwich Hill House, near North Dulwich Station. Bazaars played a large part in church life and were often elaborate two-day affairs. St Barnabas Church received its tower and Barry Road Congregational Church its spire, through such activities. It was said that the Herne Hill Methodist Church in Half Moon Lane was paid for largely through bazaars, and the zeal of the Ladies' Sewing Meeting. But how successful were the churches in bringing the gospel to the people? A survey of church attendance in 1902-3 found that only a third of the Dulwich population went to church. Of this number, 85% went to the five Anglican churches and remainder were non-conformists. In East Dulwich the figures were even more depressing: only 18% of the inhabitants went to church and of these 61% were non-conformist and 23% Anglican.

An architect's drawing of St John's, Goose Green, built in 1865 to seat 840.

OPPOSITE LEFT: Emmanuel Church, Barry Road, in use in 1874. RIGHT: St Paul's, Herne Hill, built 1858. BELOW: St Barnabas, Dulwich, 1894; the tower was added in 1908.

St Stephen's, South Dulwich from the painting by Pissaro, 1870.

ABOVE: Herne Hill Congregational Church, and the Casino House estate. The Church was built in 1904, with a capacity of 450.
LEFT: Herne Hill Methodist Church, Half Moon Lane, c1900.
INSET: St Peter's, Dulwich Common, built in 1874 for a congregation of 700.

127

ABOVE: St Clement's Friern Road, built 1885, largely at the expense of Francis Peek, who lived in Crescent Wood Road. LEFT: Methodist Church, Barry Road, opened in 1874. RIGHT: Lordship Lane Baptist Church.

PALACE OF THE PEOPLE

The Crystal Palace was everyone's favourite place from the moment it opened at Sydenham in 1854. Its slogan was 'No such shilling's worth in the world'. In 1867 it boasted picture galleries, fine arts and industrial courts, and a regular programme of events — that September its attractions included a theatre, monkey circus, fairy fountain, rifle shooting, chimpanzees and crocodiles. The concerts were famous but expensive, at 5s for the grand concert on a Saturday. Numerous organisations hired the Palace for their fêtes and drew enormous numbers, but the big international exhibitions were the real crowd-pullers. In 1862 over eighty thousand thronged to the Palace on one day for glimpses of the industrial world's exhibits.

By 1887 the Crystal Palace Company was in severe financial difficulties; the novelty was difficult to maintain. Urgent meetings of shareholders, local residents and businesses sought a solution. 'Charge less and open later' was one proposal. There was concern that the Palace would go bankrupt and bring ruin to the neighbourhood. All and sundry were urged to buy season tickets and persuade others to buy them too. Finally, a public meeting was held at the Palace, presided over by Norwood MP Mr T. Lyon Bristowe, supported by the Dulwich MP Mr Morgan Howard QC and a platform of distinguished patrons. Messages of sympathy were read from Lord Tennyson, Rev C. H. Spurgeon and the Earl of Dartmouth. It was revealed that the Palace was losing more than £10,000 per year. Concern was expressed over the possible fate of its 190 acres of gardens becoming a brickfield, and other speakers pointed out the advantage of the Palace as a means of education and amusement. If the worst happened and it closed, it was feared it would taken twenty years for the neighbourhood to be restored.

It was rescued from bankruptcy by support from the Government, no doubt conscious of the fact that 1887, Her Majesty's Golden Jubilee year, was hardly the time to allow one of her favourite projects to pass into the hands of the Receiver. The Palace management was certainly trying its hardest; despite a dull day, another crowd of over sixty thousand had passed through the turnstiles that Whit Monday. The programme offered makes incredible reading — a new picture gallery containing hundreds of pictures by British and foreign artists, three performances of a music hall entertainment in the theatre, organ recitals, band concerts by the Scots Guards and two other military bands, an orchestral concert in the morning, and in the afternoon a promenade concert by the combined bands. At 6 o'clock every seat and inch of standing room was taken in the central transept, to witness the military assault-at-arms by the instructors from the Aldershot Gymnasium. In the grounds an American circus gave six performances during the day and there was a display of the entire system of fountains. A balloon ascent was made. The big event, drawing a crowd of 40,000, was a 20-mile race on the bicycle track between J. Keen, an ex-champion 'cyclist, and Mr Rellew of Newmarket, who had three horses at his disposal to ride at will — but he also had to jump twenty hurdles. The race was exciting, and the 'cyclist won by 20 yards. The day ended with a grand display of fireworks, concluding with a great set piece 'The Bombardment of Sebastopol'.

Another notable feature of that same year were the illuminated fêtes, which took place during the summer and which had been a success the year before. They were now bigger and better. The report of the evening recalls the scene:

> 'The Rosary stands out upon its high elevation with its thousands of coloured lights and its illuminated bandstand, from which the sweet music was discoursed . . . the lines of the terrace are traced out with lamps of various colours. One of the most prominent features introduced this season is the model of the new Tower Bridge . . . which is one fourth of the size the new bridge will eventually be. At night time the bridge is illuminated with 7,000 coloured gas jets. The illuminations cover 50 acres employing 30,000 gas jets as well as electric and oil lamps.'

The Palace was Mecca to all social classes. For the lower orders, public transport facilities there were excellent, but for those who owned a carriage, the correct thing to do was drive through Dulwich, paying Mr Purdy at the toll-gate in College Road (then called Penge Road) on the way. An eye witness wrote 'I remember seeing the road from the College to the Palace full of carriages on the occasion of a Handel Festival, and in some cases postilions with white beaver hats, in the procession'. It was, of course, the fashionable way to arrive, and followed the example set by members of the Royal Family on their frequent visits, when cavalry would line the Dulwich High Street. In 1886 the Prince and Princess of Wales, accompanied by Prince Albert Victor and the Princesses Louise and Maud, drove through the village for one of the Handel concerts and 'received a most cordial greeting on the road'. The concert the Royal party attended was given by 3,000 performers and was followed by a stunning firework display.

THEIR FAVOURITE PLACE

Crystal Palace, view from the terraces 1890.

Crystal Palace during construction, 1853.

OPPOSITE ABOVE: Water tower which powered the fountains,
1890. LEFT: Helter skelter lighthouse, and RIGHT: ballooning,
c1890.

Crystal Palace, 'Topsy Turvey railway' c1900.

ABOVE: Crystal Palace, crystal fountain and great clock, 1900.

135

INDEX

All figures in *italics* refer to illustrations

*OPPOSITE ABOVE: The fairy archipelago, 1900, and BELOW:
The interior of Crystal Palace arranged for boxing tournaments.*

ENDPAPERS — East Dulwich and Peckham Rye FRONT: in
1868, BACK: in 1913 (Alan Godfrey)